BIG RIG BUSINESS STARTUP

How to Start, Run & Grow a Successful Trucking Company

By

Roy Evans

Copyrighted Material

Copyright © 2018 – **Lost River Publishing House**

All Rights Reserved.

No part of this publication may be reproduced, stored in a retrieval system or transmitted in any form or by any means, electronic, mechanical, photocopying, recording or otherwise without the proper written consent of the copyright holder, except as permitted under Sections 107 & 108 of the 1976 United States Copyright Act, without the prior written permission of the publisher.

Lost River Publishing House publishes its books and guides in a variety of electronic and print formats, Some content that appears in print may not be available in electronic format, and vice versa.

Lost River
Publishing House

Cover design

James Rodney

First Edition

TABLE OF CONTENTS

Foreword 8
Introduction: Why you should own a trucking company 11
Chapter 1: Factors to Consider 17
    Startup Factor 1: Apply for a Trucking Authority 20
    Startup Factor 2: You Need the Proper Equipment 21
    Startup Factor 3: Truck Industry 24
    Startup Factor #4: Discover the Best Customers............. 24
    Startup Factor 4: Bid the Job Boards Carefully................ 27
    Startup Factor 5: Make sure you manage your office efficiently 28
    Startup Factor 6: Be aware of your Cashflow 28
    Startup Factor 7: Select Process Agents 31
Chapter 2: Step By Step Startup Process 32
    CDL 33
    What makes someone eligible for a commercial driver's license (CDL)?... 33
    Apply for a Federal DOT and motor carrier authority numbers 34
    Obtain a Unified Carrier Registration 35
    Obtain an International Registration Plan Tag 36
    Learn about the heavy use tax regulations 36
    Get an International Fuel Tax Agreement Decal............. 36
    File a BOC-3 form 37
    Obtain a Standard Carrier Alpha Code (SCAC) 38
Chapter 3: A Business Plan for your Trucking Company 39
    Why is this single document so vital to your success?. 40

Naming your Business 42
The Six Legal Business Structures 43
    Sole Proprietorship 44
    Partnership 45
    Family partnership 47
    Corporation 47
    There are two types of corporations: the "C" and the "S" corporations 48
    Limited Liability Company (LLC) 50
    Limited Liability Partnership (LLP) 51
Apply and obtain your Employer Identification number from IRS 51
Opening a Commercial Bank Account 53
Chapter 4: Trucking Company Specific Business Plans 55
    Executive Summary 56
    Company mission 57
    Description of company 58
    Services your Business Offers 59
    Market Analysis 60
    Distinguishing Characteristics 62
    Market Share 62
    Pricing and Gross Margin Targets 63
    Competitive Analysis 63
    Regulatory Restrictions 63
    Sales and Marketing 64
    Marketing Strategy 64
    Sales Strategy 65

Your Company's Financial Goals & Future 66
Chapter-5: Finding and Buying the right Tractors 67
Chapter 6: Finance, Loans & Grants for Your Trucking Business 71
   7 Ways to find Funding for your New Business 72
   The Small Business Loan 75
      Merchant Cash Advance 77
      A working capital loan 78
      A Line of credit for your company 78
      Take out a Personal Loan 79
   What does it take to qualify for a business loan? 81
      What is LTV 81
      Adequate and Updated Insurance 82
      Minimum Revenue 84
      Credit History 84
      List of Documents you will need 85
   Grants for your trucking firm 89
     You'll need a grant proposal 90
Chapter 7: Consider Those Load Boards 94
   Invoices and Load Boards 100
Chapter 8: Freight is Freight: Or is it? 103
   A Few More Words about Loads 106
      LTL 107
      TL 107
      Air Ride Truckload 107
      Air Freight 108
      Expedited Freight Services 108

What about your competition?..108

Chapter 9: The Daily Administration of your Trucking Company 110

    The Safety Coordinator..111

    The Freight Broker 112

    Sales Representative..113

    The Dispatcher...115

Chapter- 10: Maintenance of Your Tractor........................118

    Do You Need a Shop on your Premises? 120

    How many mechanics do you need? 121

    DOT Inspections..121

Chapter 11: You and Your Drivers: How to Hire and How to Keep Them 124

    Don't be afraid to use the internet 125

    Don't embellish the job 126

    Make them feel "welcome." 126

    Develop more sophisticated pay packages.................129

    Ask your drivers what they consider is important.......129

Chapter 12: The Fuel Card..132

    How does Fuel Card work?...135

    Perks of Fuel Cards 137

        Keeping Fuel Expense under control 137

    Managing Your Fleet...137

    Improve your communication......................................138

    Miscellaneous savings 139

Chapter 13: Marketing your trucking company..................140

    Direct Mail Advertising 143

Yes, use social media too! 144
Why are you marketing? 145
Objective #1: Building a customer base 146
    Finding well-paying shippers 147
    Have you thought about the government? 150
    New customers and your cash flow 151
Objective #2: Attracting Dependable Drivers 152
    What Kind of Costs Am I Looking At? 153
    Getting your own authority 154
Conclusion 156

FOREWORD

After losing my corporate job in 2008, I went through the toughest time of my life. At the time my wife pregnant with our third child, and my monthly unemployment check wasn't enough to cover our house and two car notes. In desperation, I decided to go to a local trucking school and get my CDL.

I found my first driving job a week after I got out of school. I still remember my first paycheck was just $55 shy of what I was making at my corporate desk job. I was hysteric, I was happy, I knew this was my new found life and freedom, and no one was going to take it away from me.

Long story short, after two years of working for other companies, I decided to start my own trucking company, and I started out as an owner-operator. In 2013, I decided it was time for me to grow and time for me to get off the road and spend some time with my kids.

This was when I entered the second phase of my business life. I started to buy one tractor every three months as I was hiring great drivers that are professional, family oriented and serious about making money. By 2016 I had 12 trucks on the road, and this is also the year when my net earning passed $350,000 mark. To me, the 350K mark was always a benchmark, why? Because I knew that was the salary of the CEO of the company, I used to work for.

Last year, I received a call from a business broker, who asked me for a 10-minute meeting. He had brought an offer from a big trucking company, to buy my company. But I didn't even remotely think about selling my company. Instead, I was talking to the bank and was in the process of finalizing a loan for four new tractors with trailers. Once again, long story short, after I refused their initial offer, they came back with an offer that no reasonable man can refuse, and I consider myself a very reasonable man.

It's been almost a year since I sold my business, due to a non-compete I am not starting any new trucking business, but they never told me I couldn't write about trucking business, so here I am.

If you like the freedom and fresh air of the open road, if you like the job security and solid pay that trucking industry offers, then you need to get started now. My suggestion is even if you don't want to drive as an owner-operator, to be successful in this business, you should at least learn to drive big rigs and have your own CDL. This way, you will learn and can master the ins and outs of this business faster. Think about it, if you own a bakery, shouldn't you know how to make bread?

The income potential is truly amazing and yes, if you can hire the right people, you will not only see significant growth, high net income but the satisfaction that you don't get from many other jobs and businesses.

What I shared in this book, are the steps I went through myself, I wrote from my own experience and shared a step by step process that is easy and simple to follow, and best of all you can get started with very little funding.

INTRODUCTION: WHY YOU SHOULD OWN A TRUCKING COMPANY

There are many reasons why people decide to start their own businesses in a wide array of markets, from soap making to opening up a bakery and, yes, even trucking companies.

I'm sure you have reasons of your own for looking at the trucking industry. Don't dismiss it out of hand. Instead, consider all the benefits.

Yes, there are benefits, even though the people you've been talking to may be trying to talk you out of your crazy dream. It may sound crazy to you, but it certainly isn't to you – and you're the person who'll be putting all the puzzle pieces together.

So, what are the benefits?

First off, when you're successful your profits could be phenomenal. This industry literally generates billions of dollars in revenue. Imagine being part of an industry that generates profits like this.

It's not difficult. The advantage of this industry allows you to start small, and as you prosper and outgrow the business, it's easy to simply enlarge your firm. All you really need to do is to add drivers and trucks and to continue to invest in your firm.

Another benefit of you owning your company, maybe the biggest reason you became a truck driver, to begin with: the freedom that comes with the job. You'll still be in control of what type of freight you haul, and where you haul it. Perhaps as an owner, the freedom can be greater than ever.

And consider this advantage for a moment. You control how large your firm grows. Some investors are satisfied with just two or three trucks. Then, of course, there are other entrepreneurs discover they want to own a company with a large fleet, one with more than 100 trucks. Regardless of the size of trucking fleet you're considering, know that you can do it.

Perhaps in no other industry are customers as loyal to their vendors as in the trucking industry. While it may take some work to get a good customer base, once you have it built and you're good at what you do, they'll probably never leave you.

I don't speak about any of this lightly. I spent several decades in various positions within the industry, from company trucker to owner-operator and even a dispatcher. From these various perches, I've seen how trucking companies can work as seamlessly as a well-maintained tractor trailer. I've also witnessed how a dysfunctional company can cripple the flow of not only the freight but the profits of the firm as well.

As we walk through the different aspects of the average firm, there's one thing you'll notice. Each part of the company interacts with the other parts. This makes a smooth-running firm, but it makes describing the working of the firm difficult at times.

So, if you find a bit of overlap here and there in the description of a firm, keep that in mind. It is difficult to talk about one part of the company without talking about another.

Okay, before we start, here is a snapshot of how you can get started on owning your very own trucking company. These are the steps I will be discussing here inside this book.

Step 1 – Figure out what the name of your company will be including dba (doing business as) name along with what type of legal structure should you have for your business (S corporation, C corporation, sole proprietorship or LLC).

Step 2 – Here you need to apply for all the licenses, permits and approvals you need to operate as a trucking company from various governmental regulatory agencies.

Step 3 – Time for you to come up with a business plan which will not only help you to stay focus for both long and short terms but will also help you getting finances in the event if you need to seek for a loan for a bank.

Step 4 – If you are seeking for a loan or a grant to buy your equipment (trucks/rigs), this is where you gather up all your loan documents and apply for such loans.

Step 5 – If you came this far, you are almost to the finish line and time for you to set up your office, buy your equipment, hire drivers and other employees, you are officially in the trucking business.

Step 6 – Now that you are ready for business, time for you to find the business (loads for your trucks to carry), by subscribing to various load boards online and by contacting a few reputable freight brokers locally.

Step 7 – Marketing is the only way to grow your new business, once your company is up and running, time for you to market your business so you can grow from one rig to hundred rigs.

I will address each and every one of the above steps but not necessarily in that order, so let's get started, shall we?

CHAPTER 1: FACTORS TO CONSIDER

Are you a member of the trucking industry right now, looking around you, wondering what it would take to start your own business?

Perhaps you're a driver of a "big rig" or semi-truck now, tired of delays, bobtailing too many miles to get your next load and too many days on the road away from your family.

You may be a dispatcher who knows if, given the chance, you can get the load pick-ups and drop-offs scheduled to improve the bottom line.

But neither of you is making a move. Why?

It sounds like it's an overwhelming undertaking. It also sounds like an expensive enterprise as well. Before you dismiss the idea, yet again, consider these few, encouraging statistics about the needs and potential growth of the trucking industry within the next decade.

Most experts foresee freight revenue to grow by a stunning 75 percent within this time period. That sounds great, but what even sounds better is that the trucking industry has already earned more than 726 billion dollars in 2015 alone, the year we can find the most accurate records for.

Now that trucking company you were contemplating is sounding better and better. If done properly and you stick with it, there's no telling how much money your fledgling firm can earn.

The key to being successful is patience. You're starting small, so of course, you won't be making the money the larger truck companies will. But as a startup, you can be phenomenal. Just be sure not to let the larger, well-established companies intimidate you.

Did you know that 90 percent of all trucking companies are small fleets with six or fewer trucks? I tell you this to inspire you. You – like I always did – may have thought that most trucking companies have larger fleets. Hopefully, you're rethinking that start up now. Isn't it beginning to look possible?

When you do a bit of homework and some investigation, you may discover that it's not overwhelming at all if you break down your endeavor into simple steps. Similarly, you may be surprised how affordable launching a trucking company can be.

If you're the least bit interested in starting your own trucking company, this book is the best place to start.

Before you dig into any one topic in detail, let's look at the essential factors.

STARTUP FACTOR 1: APPLY FOR A TRUCKING AUTHORITY

Trucking company forms.

Forms. Forms. And more forms.

When you start up any business, you're going to feel as if you're drowning in paperwork. But somehow those in the truck industry seem even worse than the others. But they're necessary. And when it comes to the trucking industry, your first step is to fill out a set of these in order for you to earn trucking authority.

Have you been assigned a US DOT (United States Department of Transportation) number? If you haven't, then one of the first steps you should take is to register for a DOT number form.

This form tells the Trucking Authority what type of business you are pursuing within the trucking industry.

Keep in mind that the old MCS-150 form is now used to update existing US DOTs. It's for an existing USDOT number and not for obtaining a USDOT number. You must have a DOT number form before you can apply to obtain trucking authority.

If you go to the following site, it'll take you step-by-step of what you need to do when applying for your authority:

http://www.rtsfinancial.com/guides/license-and-permit-checklist-starting-trucking-company

STARTUP FACTOR 2: YOU NEED THE PROPER EQUIPMENT

Equipment, without a doubt, it's one of the most expensive parts of your start-up costs. It's crucial then that you get the proper equipment at the best possible price the first time around. If you begin your investment only to discover that –OOPS!!! – You made a slight mistake in this area.

You'll also need to decide if you want to buy the equipment or if it would be a better use of your money to lease. Normally, when you buy any type of large equipment for any type of business, these are your only two options.

But when you go to buy an over the road semi-truck, you have a third option. And that's to finance it as an owner-operator. If you make it clear to the salesperson you're consulting, he may try to steer you toward an owner-operator option. You'll need to make it clear to him that option is not at all what you're looking for.

You're not positioning yourself to be an owner-operator (in fact you may already be one), but you're building your own trucking firm with truckers as an integral part of your staff.
Buying equipment as you'll find is fairly straightforward. You'll learn how much is needed for

a down payment on the equipment, and then you'll take out a loan for the remainder of the cost. Once you're done making the payments, then the equipment is yours – free and clear.

Leasing the equipment is a bit more complicated than buying. But, on the plus side, leasing may allow you to make lower payments. It's a tempting option to check out, especially at the launch of the business, when money can be tight due to what seems like a myriad of start-up costs.

You can negotiate a lease that mimics a normal rental agreement. This is where you pay a monthly payment for the use of the truck. What you may not know is that you can structure a lease in several other ways as well.

Whether you buy or lease is a decision only you can make. You must decide based on your personal and business situation. Whatever you do, don't decide in haste. It could mean the difference between the success and failure of your trucking company.

STARTUP FACTOR 3: TRUCK INDUSTRY

While you're buying your equipment and planning for your business, always keep in mind that you'll need truck insurance. There is no way you can even open your doors without insurance. It's imperative you buy liability insurance, at a minimum.

This alone covers all potential damages or injuries received as the result of the commercial carrier. In addition, the lenders who are holding the titles of any of your trucks may also require even more insurance. Be sure to check with them at the time you buy your equipment.

STARTUP FACTOR #4: DISCOVER THE BEST CUSTOMERS

I can hear you now. What makes one customer better than another? If you're an owner-operator now, you're probably already finding some of your customers from the load board. We'll talk more about load boards later in this book, but for now, you're probably well aware this is where many independent operators find their load of freight for their next trip.

As wonderful as these boards can be in saving you from running your truck and making no money because you're not hauling anything, these should not be your sole focus nor a part of your long-term strategy.

A load board can be quite competitive. That means you have to bid cheap in order to get a load, very cheap sometimes. It's difficult to see good profits when you're working so close to your breakeven point.

The other aspect you need to factor into this is that a load board isn't necessarily conducive to creating long-term client relationships. Instead, they are created more for the one-off load. This means you still find yourself looking for new clients.

Yes, these boards are a necessary part at times of every trucking company. If you can, use it only while you're starting up. So, what is your alternative?

Start making smart sales calls and build your company's customer list. There's no doubt about it, building your own customer list is no walk in the park. It's a difficult job, especially if you're not established. But that doesn't mean you shouldn't try. In fact, you'll discover that customers attained and retained in this fashion will become your most profitable clients. This list will include many repeat customers who you'll have a great relationship with.

Right now, you may not realize the difference in earnings when you have a quality customer as opposed to when you rely on the load board.

A trucker told me that those who rely on the boards earn about $10,000 a month for each truck. The profits these truckers make about double that from their own corporate customers' lists – or $20,000 a month for each truck.

Let's see; each truck doubles the money made, there are fewer headaches and stress and, need we add – less work. That speaks for itself.

STARTUP FACTOR 4: BID THE JOB BOARDS CAREFULLY

In the heat of the moment and you need to find a load, you may find yourself, bidding too low on your loads.

It's a natural reaction to an environment like that. It's a fine line you're walking when you walk up to a load board. The only way to be sure you're not going actually to lose money is to know what your expenses are. Your costs which should influence your decision on placing a bid include maintenance, truck and trailer payments, fuel, truck repairs and the cost of your work.

There's also one more thing you need to take into consideration before you bid on a load, the destination or what large cities you'll need to drive through. How much is it worth to you to drive your semi-truck through the heart of New York City, a city that many truckers try to avoid at all costs.

Keep in mind too that once you drop that load off, you'll need to find another to start your way home. You don't want deadhead miles.

Startup Factor 5: Make sure you manage your office efficiently

Your company's success depends in large part on how well the back office operates. The type of office you'll need obviously will depend on the size of your business, your need for a back-office will be greater when you own a small fleet of trucks than if you're an owner-operator.

You must decide how the office should run. Review the processes you use. Make sure they all make sense, and they are the best method of performing all the tasks. Remember, perhaps more than any other business, "a trucking company runs on efficiency."

Startup Factor 6: Be aware of your Cashflow

Regardless of the type of business you run, you need to ensure you have a positive cash flow. But due to the very nature of a trucking company, maintaining a cash flow can be particularly difficult. But, it's not totally out of the question.

If it should happen to you, keep in mind that it happens to many trucking companies. The important thing is to realize that it doesn't spell the end of your business venture.

One of the biggest reasons for slow cash flow is because far too few shippers offer quick-pay. Instead of doing that, they pay on net-40 terms or even net-60.

What this means is that they have 40 or 60 days to pay. And you don't have that money you would have gotten from that load to put toward the business in that time.

Can you see the inherent problem in this? Your expenses, like fuel and repairs, can't wait 40 or 60 days to be paid. Think about it. Your truck company is growing fast. It's far too for easy to run out of cash, just when you have to get the money together for other expenses.

Hopefully, your company is growing sure and steady on a regular basis. But even if this is so, it won't take much for expenses to sneak up and get larger than your revenues. The potential ultimate problem: you have no cash and can't pull loads until those net-40 customers pay. Forty days without pulling a load is unacceptable. What about your regular customers? You're leaving them high and dry.

Don't expect them to hang out. They're going out to look for a trucking company that can deliver (no pun intended!) You can remedy this by using a type of financing called "freight factoring." This method actually offers you an advance payment on your slow-paying freight bills.

If you use this method, you won't need to wait for those 40 to 60 days to get paid. With freight factoring, you can get money immediately from the factoring company. In this way, you can not only cover your expenses but take on new loads at the same time.

STARTUP FACTOR 7: SELECT PROCESS AGENTS

A process agent is your representative regarding your court papers. You'll need to have such an agent in which your business operates.

His/her role is to be your proxy if there are court papers to be served to your company in a state other than the one your company is registered.

CHAPTER 2: STEP BY STEP STARTUP PROCESS

If you didn't pay much attention to the number of rules and regulations surrounding the trucking industry, you're beginning to get an idea now. Whatever business you decide to start has its own set of regulations.

Of course, these rules, whether in the trucking business or any other one, are meant to keep your customers safe and to ensure your employees are treated fairly. Before you can turn the key to your big rigs, there are several government rules and regulations that you must satisfy – and stay up-to-date. Here is a quick list and a short description of a few of the vital ones you'll need to get your authority – your ability to haul freight.

CDL

That seems obvious, doesn't it? But it is indeed the first step you must take in order to even begin establishing a business. Of course, this goes on the assumption that, at least for the first year, you'll be one of the drivers on your fleet.

First, you need to be prepared for undergoing an extensive background check. Beyond that, you'll need to take a written permit exam, CDL training and then take the driving test.

WHAT MAKES SOMEONE ELIGIBLE FOR A COMMERCIAL DRIVER'S LICENSE (CDL)?

You need to be a minimum of 18 years old. But, that age only allows you to drive within the state the license is issued. If you want to drive over-the-road, you need to be 21 years old.

One of the concepts you need to factor in your driving, as well as hiring drivers, is that each state has its own set of rules and regulations with regard to CDLs. To discover what your state requires of you, you'll need to obtain a manual for this license at your local department of motor vehicles.

Apply for a Federal DOT and Motor Carrier Authority Numbers

These are absolutely required so your company will have the ability to transport freight throughout the entire United States. The US Department of Transportation number you'll be issued is used to keep track of your company's safety record as well as your compliance with their regulations.

The motor carrier number usually referred to simply as the MC, is recognized as an "operating authority." This number identifies not only the type of trucking business you own but also the kinds of goods you're allowed to move. The average application fee for MC is around $300.

You can get both numbers simply by registering your company with the Federal Motor Carrier Safety Administration commonly called the FMCSA.

In order to obtain both of them, you must complete the Motor Carrier Identification Report, or MCS-150 and Safety Certification. But wait, that's not all you need. Once you file, the application will be reviewed by the FMCSA. Included in this step is a "mandated dispute period." What's this? The FMCSA posts your application to the Federal Register for ten business days. This gives time for anyone who might contest your application to do so.

For more information, visit the FMCSA's website, https://www.fmcsa.dot.gov/.

OBTAIN A UNIFIED CARRIER REGISTRATION

You may hear this called by its initial the UCR. This registration verifies insurance coverage has not lapsed in each state in which you operate. You register for this through your USDOT and MC numbers. You can learn more about the UCR by visiting your state's DOT website.

OBTAIN AN INTERNATIONAL REGISTRATION PLAN TAG

You can get an IRP license plate from your company's home state. While it's issued by the state in which your company is grounded, this allows your trucks to run in all states, and in most of the Canadian provinces. You'll have an annual fee associated with this plate. For instructions for applying for the plates, go to your state's DOT website.

LEARN ABOUT THE HEAVY USE TAX REGULATIONS

Planning on hauling a truck that weighs more than 55,000 pounds? If you are, then be prepared to be subject to the heavy use tax regulations. This means you'll need to pay taxes on these runs. In order to comply with this, you'll need to file a 2290 tax once a year. To get more information about this visit the government's website, www.irs.gov.

GET AN INTERNATIONAL FUEL TAX AGREEMENT DECAL

This is also called an IFTA agreement, and it was created to simplify your mandate of reporting your company's fuel used in the states on the mainland of the country as well as several Canadian provinces. This regulation means your firm only needs one fuel license. It also requires you to file fuel tax returns on a quarterly basis. To find more specifics about what's required in your state, visit its DOT website.

FILE A BOC-3 FORM

This form can be obtained through the FMCSA and designates a person in each state in which your firm operates to act as a legal "process agent." Let's say that your company is based in Missouri and you find yourself sued by an individual in Georgia.

You'll need to retain an attorney who is registered in Georgia who can receive the legal complaint as well as follow up on it in working closely with you and your attorney. You can discover what your state requires in obtaining a BOC-3, check out the FMCSA website at:

www.fmcsa.dot.gov.

OBTAIN A STANDARD CARRIER ALPHA CODE (SCAC)

This code is privately controlled. That's used to identify the various transportation companies. If you're planning on moving loads for the military or government or hauling international or intermodal loads, you'll need this. Get more information on this through the following website:

http://www.nmfta.org/(X(1)S(boqtwizydte2u20bk4mwqd1q))/?AspxAutoDetectCookieSupport=1

CHAPTER 3: A BUSINESS PLAN FOR YOUR TRUCKING COMPANY

We've avoided the topic long enough. If you're leaning toward running a trucking business, this is one of the must-have documents your investors will want to see. While many individuals cringe at the thought of writing a business plan, it needn't be so frightening and certainly not as difficult as you believe.

The key to building a coherent, persuasive plan is to take one step at a time. Below is a quick walk through the parts of a business plan aimed at getting funding and keeping you on track for your own trucking company.

WHY IS THIS SINGLE DOCUMENT SO VITAL TO YOUR SUCCESS?

It's the most effective way to convey the goals of your company – as well as it's stability from the ground up. You're going to use this as an owner's manual for building your dream. But it's also your most effective way to convey to your potential investors why your dream is not only feasible, but you're serious about manifesting it into reality.

You could outsource this document to some faceless freelance writer you've found on the web, but before you do that give it a bit more consideration. The actual writing of the plan may be the most pivotal event in your startup company.

When you write the business plan, it provides you with a breather of sorts from the minutia of the daily operations. It allows you, in effect, to get a clear view of the big picture.

Some of the factors that you'll get the crisper view include the following:

What do you believe are the greatest strengths in your marketplace?
Where do you want your company to be five years from now?
How are you different from your competitors?
How do you plan to achieve the growth you're aiming for?

Before you create your business plan, even before you do any serious dreaming about creating your business, you'll be faced with the question: What type of corporate business structure do you plan to use?

You probably knew that this question would eventually pop up. You knew you'd have to confront it and choose the best for you. Perhaps you weren't quite ready to be asked about it so early in the startup steps.

If you haven't researched this topic yet, now's as good as time as any to familiarize yourself with the six different structures. Of course, before you make a decision do more research, you should also include discussions with your accountant and attorney. At the very least, when you enter these discussions, you'll have some idea of what your professional consultants are explaining.

NAMING YOUR BUSINESS

This is the first thing on the list for a number of reasons. First, branding will be critical to your business. You have to be able to stand out from rest of your competitors; customers need to know why you are different, and superior to your competition in order to give your new trucking company a viable chance to survive and succeed. So now you need a great name that stands out.

Here are some things to consider. Your name must be relevant in some way to who you are, your business, or your location. It needs to be connected to what you do. Your name should be short enough to be easily remembered. When you choose your name, it has to be unique, meaning not being used by any other company.

Google the name you have chosen and see if another business pops up, if not you are in great shape. Checking your business name with the Patent and Trade Mark Office to ensure that it is unique is another sure-fire method. Once you find the unique name that you want, it is time to buy the domain for the name of your business.

For example, if you have named you trucking company "Quality Trucking," you want to buy the domain "QualityTrucking.com" you might want to buy other top-level domains or TDLs.

Examples of other ones are ".net" or ".biz." buying these can prevent others from being able to use your name with these TDLs. Most domain sellers such as GoDaddy.com offer packages that allow you to purchase the domain with multiple TDLs.

THE SIX LEGAL BUSINESS STRUCTURES

Sole Proprietorship

Partnership

C Corporation (C Corp)

S Corporation (S Corp)

Limited Liability Company (LLC)

Limited Liability Partnership (LLP)

Each of these six options has their own advantages and disadvantages. The best one for you is, as always, based on your circumstances and your personal preferences.

SOLE PROPRIETORSHIP

Sole proprietorship dominates U.S. small businesses. Approximately 80 percent of all businesses are formed within this legal structure. This type of structure is self-explanatory.

Choose this structure and by law become the only owner of the company. Its popularity is probably at least partially due to the fact that it's the least expensive legal set up. Typically, there is no formal startup date. Your sole proprietorship begins the day you start earning money with your business.

This appears to be the structure of choice for owner-operators who are starting up a fleet of trucks.

A sole proprietorship has disadvantages, of course. The largest problem with this is the concept of liability. If you should experience an accident, you may be liable for tremendously large sums of money beyond your ability to pay, between vehicle damage and medical expenses.

As an aside, that's a perfect example as well to illustrate the need for bobtail insurance. There's a reason why large trucking firms carry millions of dollars in liability insurance. If covered properly by insurance, losing everything you own in this circumstance would be highly improbable.

PARTNERSHIP

The partnership is recognized under the business law when two or more individuals own a company. Each individual is taxed separately as if they were a sole proprietor of the business. Similarly, each member of the partners can be held liable for the actions of the other.

While it takes a few legal hoops to jump through when you form it, it would be advisable before you and your partner launch the business, that you form a written agreement of some type. Your attorney can help you create this agreement. There are several good factors which would make this type of corporate structure advantageous. Each partner has access to extra startup capital.

But more than that, when the partnership is created in a trucking firm, you have a potential co-driver to help you cover more miles. When choosing a partner, one of your major concerns should be the ability of the two of you to get along, not only in a professional way but also socially.

In an ideal partnership, each person should be able to bring some unique talent to the firm, a talent the other individual doesn't have. In other words, their talents should complement each other. For example, if you're strong in finances, you may want to search for a partner who is rich in mechanical expertise.

Each should bring something to the table that the other person lacks. One may be strong in financial matters, for example, while the other may have mechanical expertise.

There are several specialized partnerships that include, but not necessarily limited to the following:

FAMILY PARTNERSHIP

There's no reason not to have family members as partners, as long as you can separate family from business. You need to know, though, the Internal Revenue Service recognizes family partnership only each if partner meets specific IRS criteria.
In a husband-wife partnership, spouses can share the operation of a business including the profits and losses. And they, unlike some partnerships, don't need to have signed a formal partnership agreement.

CORPORATION

A corporation differs from the other structures we've already reviewed in several different areas. According to the law, a corporation is an entity completely separate from its owners, as well as its shareholders and employees. The law regarding incorporating firms vary from state to state, as well as the cost. In some states, under certain circumstances, it may cost as little as a couple of hundreds of dollars compared to several thousands of dollars in other states.

In addition to the fees to create the corporation, if you choose this route requires you to file numerous forms, records, and other paperwork. Not only that, but it also mandates that your corporation have an annual meeting of all those who have a stake in the business.

This usual means a meeting all individuals who own stock in the business. You've heard, no doubt, of some firms, incorporate in states other than their headquarters. While many firms do this, it can open your firm up to potential problems. If you're an owner-operator, you may be tempted to create this type of business. Most legal experts agree it's not a great fit for them because it's just too costly compared to any benefits you may receive from it.

THERE ARE TWO TYPES OF CORPORATIONS: THE "C" AND THE "S" CORPORATIONS

The "C" corporation, in addition to being an entity of its own, pays taxes on the income it earns. That is to say that the driver becomes an employee of the corporation and should receive a paycheck, just like all the other employees of the firm. If the driver refuses to take a paycheck, the money becomes a dividend and becomes subject to being taxed twice. At the corporate level, it gets taxed and then again at the individual level.

The "S" corporation, the second option keeps the driver as an employee and he is obligated to report the income of the corporation on his personal tax return. The income is taxable at the individual level and, unlike its sister structure, there is no issue with double taxation.

Not only that, but the earnings aren't subject to any potential self-employment taxation. The only caveat in this scenario is that the paycheck of the driver must be of a reasonable nature. If it's too high in comparison to other drivers, the IRS will notice and consider auditing your firm.

It's a tempting corporate structure for an owner-operator to adopt. These individuals see it as a way to avoid liability while protecting their own assets.

It's also attractive to lessen the taxation. The court system does not accept this structure as one an owner-operator should be establishing. And the court system is the final judge. It's possible, should you face a lawsuit, a court would disqualify this structure, leaving the driver solely responsible for the firm's debts, taxes, penalties and yes, of course, lawsuits.

LIMITED LIABILITY COMPANY (LLC)

Also called an LLC, this legal structure provides protection for its owners. The profits of an LLC flow through the owner's personal income tax, so there is no concern about any double taxation. This is considered by some because it's more flexible than a C corporation and much simpler.

Here again, this is probably, not the structure that an owner-operator should adopt. Each state treats this type of structure differently. To illustrate this point, consider a firm which set up an LLC in Wisconsin. The firm experiences an accident in another state. The firm's liability protection is up to debate.

Limited Liability Partnership (LLP)

This business structure is usually referred to as an LLP and like other similar structures, can be complicated and expensive to establish. It, as you might guess, is not recommended for owner-operators.

Apply and Obtain Your Employer Identification Number from IRS

EIN or Employer Identification number is essentially a social security or tax identification number but for your business. IRS and many other governmental agencies can identify your business via this unique nine-digit number.

Remember you will not need this number if you choose to be a sole proprietorship for your business.

It is simple to apply, either you can do it yourself or get your accountant to apply for you, but the process is simple, you fill out the form SS-4, which can be filed online, via Fax or via mail.

Here is a link to IRS website where you can download or fill out the form online.

https://www.irs.gov/businesses/small-businesses-self-employed/how-to-apply-for-an-ein

OPENING A COMMERCIAL BANK ACCOUNT

This is one important step, but it can only be done after you have a fully executed article of incorporation which has been approved by the state, and you have an EIN assigned by the IRS.

Once you have these two documents, you should be able to go to any commercial bank and open your first commercial checking account.

But remember to check and understand various types of commercial checking account fees, you want to find a bank that offers free or almost free commercial checking account because some larger banks can charge you hundreds of dollars each month depending on how many transactions you do. Make sure to ask and shop around before you sign on the dotted line.

Next step would be to go to your local city and county business licensing office and find out what type of business and regulatory licenses you are required to have. It should take a few days to get your licenses and permits in place, and then you are finally and officially in business.

CHAPTER 4: TRUCKING COMPANY SPECIFIC BUSINESS PLANS

No doubt about it. Due to the nature of a business plan, each one is unique. Unfortunately, there is no golden formula to the perfect plan that would guarantee funding as well as a solid roadmap to success.

The good news, thanks to the internet, you don't have to write this alone. For a small monthly fee, you can buy software that will guide you through this project.

Check out the following site, https://www.liveplan.com/ to learn more about this aid. I've never used it so I can't give it my recommendation, but before you pull your hair out, you should at least check it out.

You may want to check out another internet site that may be able to help you. It's a veritable treasure trove of business plans for just about any industry imaginable, including trucking. The site is:

https://www.bplans.com/transportation_business_plan_templates.php

Regardless of whether you use either of these sites, I've provided you with a general outline of what's involved in an effective and complete business plan for a trucking firm.

EXECUTIVE SUMMARY

This is the first section your investors and banker will see, and it's exactly what it claims to be: a summary of your plan in general. For this reason, this may be the last item you want to write, after you've pulled all the facts and options together.

In this section, your readers will also want to see your idea of your future plans. And, oh yes. Be sure to include in this section *why* you know that your firm will meet its goals.

You don't need to be overly wordy in this section. It should be a quick read, but it does need to have good information in there. This may sound like it puts pressure on you, but even your potential investors won't read much farther than this if they don't find this compelling. In a nutshell, your business plan summary needs to provide a quick synopsis of the following four goals.

COMPANY MISSION

Products and services you plan on providing
Performance highlights
Financial information

Future plans

DESCRIPTION OF COMPANY

In this section, your investors will be expecting to read about the history and background of your business. Your investors want to know the overarching mission of your company. They also need to be assured that your company is different from the competition. If you can offer a service or a perk to customers that Joe's Trucking in the next town isn't, then you'll have a better shot at success than other firms.

It's in this section that you'll be including key facts about your proposed firm. If it's already a business then, your potential investors will want to know the overview of your current business, including the owners of it, the year it was incorporated as well as where you conduct your business and the states in which you currently registered.

This is also the section in which, should you have any employees, outline your current organization as well as the roles your employees play and their responsibilities.

Take some time as well to talk about your company's successes in this area.

Don't be afraid to promote your company's advantages over its competitors, such as new clients. Describe the growth of your fleet and anything else you feel is significant, and definitely any other success you've experienced recently.

SERVICES YOUR BUSINESS OFFERS

This section is self-explanatory. What are the services your company provides – or your proposed company will offer. Basically, the readers of your business plan are waiting for you to tell them how you're meeting (or planning to meet) the needs of your customers.

Let me give you an example. A trucking company working out of Atlanta explained that it hauls flatbed loads. Why? The answer is quite simple. The southeastern region of the United States has a longer "construction season" than, say the Midwest.

This region of the country also has a large and prosperous timber industry. If you're able to include the demographics of your customers, this will only serve to bolster your argument.

You can also include in this section the details about your pricing structure, the specific material you haul and what kind of industries you serve.

MARKET ANALYSIS

While this section isn't considered to be a trap, not even a quiz, it could be a real eye-opener, not just for you, but also for your potential investors. This section illustrates your knowledge about industry trends, as well as customer needs. It also explains your plans on capitalizing on them.

It would do you well in this section to state the facts as you've researched them to be. You'll want to show your investors that not only do have access to a broad range of data, but you can interpret it and be willing to act on it.

This can buoy confidence in your potential investors and fact may swing them your way. With this information and a convincing interpretation of them, you can show your readers what you can expect in the trucker company and that you'll have no problems succeeding in a crowded trucking market.

What type of topics should you insert in this section? Below are some of the topics you should include.

US Small Business Administration.
Industry Description and Outlook

Here the SBA suggests that you explain how large your segment of the trucking industry is. You'll want to include who the major carriers here as well as the major shippers.

What are your ideal demographics? In other words, what's your company's "sweet spot?" Your company can narrow this market, target your sweet spot, and market to customers that can provide you with the greatest returns. If you can do this, your company will certainly be the brightest star in a sky already filled with stars.

DISTINGUISHING CHARACTERISTICS

In this section, you'll want to explain what the critical needs are of this sweet spot of customers.

How do you plan on fulfilling their needs?
What is the size of your primary target market?
In this section, estimate the size of your target market as well as any additional details you know about them and their needs.

MARKET SHARE

Your investors are asking you to put in this section how much business you expect to gain within a specific period of time. While they know that you are providing conjecture, it should be predictions based on current trends and what type of growth you've seen within the industry as well as your own business.

Your readers will also want you to provide a strong, logical argument for your conclusions.

PRICING AND GROSS MARGIN TARGETS

Inform your readers of your company's pricing structure, its margins and if you believe that any discounts would improve your growth.

COMPETITIVE ANALYSIS

This section illustrates that you've researched your competitors by describing their strengths and weaknesses.

REGULATORY RESTRICTIONS

What your readers want to read here is how government regulations affect your business. Be honest. Include if you need to maintain certain regulations like hours of service for your drivers and current fuel emissions' guidelines. Here again, your potential investors want you to grab your crystal ball and predict – with the knowledge you're armed with – how any future restrictions may affect your business and its growth.

SALES AND MARKETING

As you're reading the steps of a business plan, I hope you're beginning to get a feel for how one aspect of the plan builds upon the one before it. This section uses the information you gathered in the previous section to create an effective marketing strategy to help you gain market share.

First, to make this a bit less daunting, you'll want to split this into two broad categories. The first is your marketing strategy and the second is a sales strategy.

MARKETING STRATEGY

Let's dive into the marketing strategy first. In this part of the plan, you'll outline your best thoughts on how to retain your loyal customer base, while at the same time drawing in new customers. You investors will want to know how you plan on promoting your services. They'll be searching for the channels you plan to use.

What do I mean by that? Are you planning on promoting your services on social media or through trade publications or even email lists? Another topic some truck owners put in this section is if there are any major purchases in the near future, or if you believe you'll be targeting a specific region with your marketing efforts.

SALES STRATEGY

Here, the investors want you to talk about the vision you hold for your sales force. In other words, they want to know if you'll be adding any sales associates. On the flip side, are you going to use independent agents, in-house, or some mix. In effect, the questions include the process of your plan for calling on your prospects.

One final thing should be included in this sales strategy section. Tell your investors about your process for contacting these prospects. While you're talking about all these items, be sure to include the closing rate of your sales team and how that affects your company's financial goals.

Your Company's Financial Goals & Future

In this portion of your business plan, you'll provide your readers with financial statements and other information which illustrate how your company will meet its financial goals. You'll need to include basic financial statements like your profit and loss document, cash flow as well as your company's balance sheet and your sales forecast.

But more than that you'll need to be persuasive on your company's performance within the next five years. Be sure that your financial projections square with any financing requests you make to boost your business's growth.

Of course, your business plan doesn't need to follow these exact steps. But these are the common items. To truly succeed, you must remember that your plan needs to be unique. It needs to deal with your specific conditions and your personal goals.

CHAPTER-5: FINDING AND BUYING THE RIGHT TRACTORS

In US and Canada, there are five big name truck manufacturers that you have to pick one from.

1. Freightliner – The top-selling semi-truck in the US is Freightliner, they sell well over 200,000 trucks each year.
2. Kenworth – PACCAR is the parent company that owns both Kenworth and Peterbilt. Both

brands combined, they sell around 150,000 trucks a year

3. Peterbilt – In some ways, Peterbilt is more of an iconic trucking brand then Kenworth, even though they both are owned by the same company.
4. International – Navistar International is another iconic American company that started in 1902, they sell around 115,000 units a year.
5. Volvo – Volvo is the Swedish brand that is also known for their cars and SUV's. Even though they less little less 100,000 trucks average a year in the US; they are the second largest heavy-duty truck producer in the entire world.

If you are looking to buy brand new rigs, a new tractor should run you around $110,000 -$125,000 depending on the brand and how big of a sleeper cab you want in it. Then there is another $25,000 to as high as $45,000 for a new trailer.

But before you go out buy both, if you need to analyze your business model. If you are just haling trailers for other companies, then you most likely won't need your own trailer. So it is a good idea to analyze load boards first and see which type of loads attract you the most.

You may also need to consider buying a good used tractor and save a lot of money. Just to give you an example, I just found a 2015 Kenworth T680 sleeper tractor in mint condition with 500K miles for $64,500. I am sure I can negotiate the price down by a couple of thousands from the asking price. As you can see, that is almost 50% less than buying a new tractor.

Here are a few good sites that you can check and compare prices before deciding to buy any of your equipment.

http://www.tbg-truckbuyersguide.com/search-results-truck.asp?TruckTypeID=1

http://www.bigrigtt.com/truck-sales/

https://www.commercialtrucktrader.com/Tractor-Trucks-For-Sale/search-results?category=Tractor%7C2008002 http://www.50000trucks.com/Kenworth-trucks-for-sale.aspx

CHAPTER 6: FINANCE, LOANS & GRANTS FOR YOUR TRUCKING BUSINESS

Startup Expenses	
Corporation setup	$1,000.00
Permits, licenses & Fees	$1,200.00
Insurance (Down Payment)	$2,500.00
Home Office Setup	$1,000.00
Load Board Memberships	$500.00
1 New Rig (Without Bank loan)	$125,000.00
Fuel (First Month out of pocket)	$6,500.00
Logo and other Design work	$1,500.00
Misc. Maintenance	$1,800.00
Startup Cash	$5,000.00
Advertising & Marketing	$1,500.00
Total Startup Expenses	**$147,500.00**

You know your passion says, "Go for it! Start a trucking company".

Your wallet, however, screams back, "Are you crazy? I'm empty now, how are you going to pay for it?"

Which one do you listen to and how do you decide?

Thankfully, you may be able to please both, your passion as well as your finances.

7 Ways to find Funding for your New Business

Sometimes you just have to be little creative when it comes to finding "Money" for your business.

Here are just a few ideas that may help you find the funding you need for your new business.

1. Your own savings/401K etc.
2. A home equity line of credit (this is how I got started with mine)
3. Family funding (where your parents, siblings help you with a personal loan)
4. Create a partnership with people that have the money
5. Crowdfunding
6. Applying for a small business loan at your local bank
7. Applying for a federal grant for your business

For this brainstorming part, you first need to sit down, take a piece of paper, try to analyze each and every option and then see which one seems more doable for you. You can even do a mix and match here. For example, you need $100,000 to buy your first truck, but you only have $50,000 to borrow from your 401K, one idea is to ask one or two like-minded friends or family to come in as a 50% partner, where you hold 50% of the business, the other two gets 25% each.

As for crowdfunding, I have never done it, but have seen it done. You can make a list of 10-20 people that you know. Ask each of them for an investment of $10,000 for a 7% stake in your company. If 10 of them agree, you will have $100,000, and you only gave out 70% of your business. The remaining 30% is still yours for FREE.

You just have to be creative, remember when there is a strong will power to achieve something, there is always a way to get there.

As for applying for a loan at the bank is the hardest of all other methods I outlined above. In the event you have no other option but to apply for a loan, you do have to do some research first.

If you do even a casual search on the internet, you'll soon discover that you may qualify either for a loan or better yet, a grant for your firm. A loan, as you well know, must be paid back upon the terms set up by the entity loaning your firm the money. A grant, on the other hand, doesn't require any paying back of the money. It's yours free and clear, as long as you use it for the purposes you declared originally.

Initially, the money in the form of a grant sounds good. But don't dismiss the possibility of a loan. There may come a time during the life of your business; you may find yourself short of cash. And when you do, you'd be wise to seek out a loan from a reputable bank or other entity.

You may find you need extra cash in order to repair or even replace a truck. That's just one example. I'm sure you've already run through all the worst-case scenarios of your business while you've been researching and planning.

Before you apply for a loan, you need to review your status in these areas of your financial life: your credit history, business history, the cash flow of your business, and the repayment time-frame of the loan you're being offered. All of these will factor together to determine how large a loan you can borrow, the interest rate on the money, as well as the time period you have in which to repay it.

THE SMALL BUSINESS LOAN

One of the most common, and without a doubt, the best-known method of gaining money to launch your business is the startup business loan. The key factor in a loan like this is that all the partners in the business take a portion of the financial risk. Usually, every person that owns 20 percent or more of a startup loan is liable for a percentage of the loan.

Sometimes, the definition of "partners" shifts. In some cases, each individual who is in a key management position within your business is liable for the loan – even if they don't own a portion of the business. Of course, if your trucking firm is structured as a sole proprietorship, then, you're the sole person who is legally responsible for paying the loan back.

While that sounds daunting, it really isn't as ominous as it sounds. Normally it's difficult to understand the fluctuations of the marketplace for a startup business loan. After all, if there were no risks to being an entrepreneur, everyone would be out there busy, setting up one of their own.

Consider this, though. Many market experts say this is one of the best times not only to start a business but also find funding for it. They say that if you look around you, you'll discover there are more "tried and true" choices for these loans than ever before.

You'll discover that the vast majority of startup loans are typically backed by any number of government agencies as well as private lenders. For the most part, the average interest rate falls around or below 10 percent.

This can be the perfect option if you're seeking money in order to buy more than one truck at a time due to expansion or for any other area you're planning to expand and improve.

Amazingly, you can get loans with repayment terms of upwards of 20 years, and you'll be pleased how large a loan you can obtain, depending on your financial history.

MERCHANT CASH ADVANCE

This type of "loan" seems to be gaining in popularity among small business owners, regardless of the specialty of their firms. A merchant cash advance may help you in the pinch of an unexpected financial emergency. But you need to enter into this agreement with your eyes wide open, understanding exactly what the terms of the transaction are.

The main draw for business owners is that you can get money, basically few questions asked, without going through a credit check.

A WORKING CAPITAL LOAN

You may be less familiar with this type of loan. I've talked to many small business owners who were totally surprised to be offered a loan with terms of a working capital loan. In this type of situation, you don't put up a piece of equipment as collateral. Instead, the lender considers your regular income as what's at stake if you fail to repay it.

A LINE OF CREDIT FOR YOUR COMPANY

If you're searching for a loan without the prospect of pledging any piece of equipment as collateral, then you might want to consider a line of credit. While interests will vary from one lender to the next, I know of one company that has received $200,000.

TAKE OUT A PERSONAL LOAN

Yes, it should make you quiver in your boots. But people do it all the time. And taking out a personal loan for your business isn't the risk you may at first believe. And certainly isn't as risky as your family and friends may warn you.

As long as you've done your homework and have a solid business plan, then you can be confident your trucking firm will succeed.

Additionally, depending on the circumstances, the risks that normally accompany using your personal credit are outweighed by the possible advantages. You have to remember that start-up businesses of all kinds seem to run into hurdles when attempting to qualify for financing. The main hurdle? Your company isn't old enough to have a credit history long enough to satisfy any lender.

So, knowing that piece of information should give you a bit of confidence going into the process.

Another reason you may want to consider taking out a personal loan for your business is that it's a shorter process. That's right. From the moment you apply for a personal loan to the moment the money is in your bank account is a short time compared to the time between applying and receiving a business loan.

The bottom line is that approval for a personal loan is for the most part based on strong personal credit and low credit use. With regard to a business loan, approval depends on your personal credit and several other qualifying criteria. Given this situation, it takes the lenders longer to review all the extra information that goes into a business loan. Before you run out to your local bank, check out the following disadvantages and dangers of taking out a personal loan for your business:

- The loan might not cover everything you need.

- Depending on why you need the loan, the largest amount you can borrow based on your personal credit may still fall short of your business needs.

- You've just increased your personal liability

- Personal loans have a higher APR or annual percentage rate

What does it take to qualify for a business loan?

You may find it difficult to qualify for the first loan for which you apply. That's not necessarily a reflection of you or your business. It much more mirrors the fact that the truck firms which haul freight are labeled "high-risk industries" among the lending companies and banks. That, however, doesn't mean it's impossible.

Below are just a few of the most common hurdles a trucking firm needs to overcome before it can sign on the dotted line.

What is LTV

One thing to keep in mind, all banks and commercial lenders do have to follow certain guideline that is set by federal and state banking authorities. Also, every bank will look at something call LTV (Loan to Value) ratio of the property or business you are looking to buy.

LTV is essentially where banks look at the actual value of the business you are looking to buy or lease and how much of that value they can loan you.

Adequate and Updated Insurance

You'd be amazed at how many owners, especially novices, get tripped up here – nearly right from the gate. It's not enough to have enough insurance on all of your trucks but check out to make sure you have a suitable amount on your inventory as well. This aids you because it lessens your business risk, but it's something that lenders scrutinize. Lenders feel safer and more at ease lending to a firm that has adequate insurance.

Before you buy insurance, make sure to get at least two to three quotes from three different but reputable insurance companies to make sure you get the best coverage for the lowest price.

Here are the top ten insurance companies that are well-known in the commercial trucking industry.

- State Farm.
- Allstate.
- Nationwide.
- Farmers Insurance.
- Travelers.
- The Hartford.
- Liberty Mutual.
- 1st Guard.
- esurance

- Progressive

MINIMUM REVENUE

Another factor lenders check is the minimum amount of money your firm brings in on a monthly basis. This is the best indication these financial institutions have when they decide what type of position your firm is in to repay the loan. Typically, the lenders consider an income of no less than $8,000 a month as their solid rock bottom minimum.

CREDIT HISTORY

The company's credit history also plays a role in whether your business gets accepted for a loan. First, they'll look at how long your firm has been doing business. For the most part, you need to be a working firm for at least six months. This is the shortest length of time that they can accurately assess your firm's credit history. But don't worry, if you are just starting out, most banks will just look at your personal credit history and financials.

While this may seem like you're expected to jump over many hurdles, if taken one by one, these factors don't seem so overwhelming. The good news is that if you meet all of these criteria, the odds are on your side that you'll not only receive the loan, but the lenders will get it to you quickly. If for any reason, you can't meet all of the requirements and are denied a loan, perhaps you should take out a loan using your personal line of credit.

LIST OF DOCUMENTS YOU WILL NEED

Let's look at the list of documents you will need to get ready to submit to your bank. Some of these items I will mention here may not be on your bank's checklist but do gather them anyway as it will make you look more professional and business-like.

1. You need to get copies of at least last three years of personal tax returns, make sure the copies are signed.

2. Your resume (they may not even ask you for it, but remember the person that may approve your loan may never meet you but this way at least he or she gets to see who you are and how qualified you are it always helps)

3. Copy of your Corp. Articles, (yes you have to get this done before you even apply for your loan)

4. Personal financial statement for all Corporate Officers or members, make sure to sign it, if you are married and file joint tax returns than your wife needs to have one prepared for her as well or you can make a joint personal financial statement for

both of you and make sure to both sign that document.

5. Copy of the commercial appraisal/valuation of the equipment you want to buy.

6. Copy of signed purchase agreement (If applicable)

7. Copy of your EIN (Employer's Identification Number) issued by the IRS

8. Copy of all member/partner's Driver's licenses and social security cards

9. A well thought out and expertly written Business Plan (not a store bought one or copy-pasted one, one that is written for your specific business, get help if you need to, but this has to be a well thought out plan, do it like your life depends on it trust me on this.)

10. Last but the least the loan application all filled out, use a computer and printer if possible, if not write very clearly, so it is easy to read.

11. A cover letter addressed to the loan department where you describe what is in the package and thanking them for reviewing your loan application and lastly tell them where they easily reach you if they need further help or other documents from you, it just makes you look more professional.

Now, remember to organize these papers with nice tabs and in a binding folder where anyone can open the folder, looking at the tabs, they can go directly to that specific section.

If you are applying for an SBA specific business loan, then SBA may also give you a loan package with some more documents and forms to fill out, but they will mostly ask for the same as I just mentioned.

But yes they will have you fill out many more forms, and don't worry you do not have to visit SBA office separately they work through your local banks so the loan officer you deal with will furnish you all of that.

GRANTS FOR YOUR TRUCKING FIRM

We've mentioned at the beginning of this chapter that if you searched, you'd be able to find a grant or two for your trucking firm.

A grant, of course, is money from a third party who is willing to give you money in order for you to either reduce your startup or operating costs. Grants, as you can guess aren't as easy to find, but they are available. So, if you have an interest in obtaining one, then you'll have to approach your search with both time and patience.

On the plus side, though, you can kick-start your search by visiting the website

http://www.grants.gov

In addition to that, check out the state in which your headquarters are. Very often the states have an office that's dedicated to assessing and administrating grants

More than that though, you should also look for private grants. Again, that will require some research on your part. The best research is to return to these sites on a regular basis. If you visit one time and they have nothing that fits your needs, wait a month or two if you can. These funds are typically updated on a regular business.

You'll need a grant proposal

Writing a grant proposal may sound as intimidating as writing a business plan. But once you break the sections down, you'll discover that it isn't at all that difficult to write. If, though, even after that, keep in mind there are individuals out there who write this type of proposal for a living. But it comes with a price tag, very often a percentage of the grant itself.

If you have anyone on your payroll who can write, he can probably do this. Requirements for grants vary from one to another of course, but generally speaking just about every grant has some core questions.

For example, every grantor needs to know why you need the money, in other words, what is the grant going to be used for. Secondly, you'll have to show them why you and your firm deserve the grant. Keep in mind that you are undoubtedly not the only person vying for the money. While I've already mentioned that hiring a grant writer isn't necessary, you still may want to give it some thought.

If you hire a professional grant writer, you can be satisfied that he knows the phrases and examples to show the grantor that can almost guarantee your company is receiving at least a portion of what you're requesting.

Here's a quick overview of some of the best methods for funding your startup. It is, by no means, a complete listing. But it will help you begin to think about possibilities.

Type of Business Loan	Description	Ideal circumstances
Startup equipment financing	Your business equipment is collateral. Among the lowest interest rates	Perfect for expenses such as trucking companies and some restaurant startups`
Business credit cards	Gives you access to a revolving cred line that can pay for incoming purchases	Those owners with strong personal credit
Credit line builders	The finance company will approve your firm for a set of	New owners with strong personal credit and are well disciplined in their

	credit cards which will go toward building good business credit.	spending habits.
Small Business Administration loans	Usually smaller amounts, backed by the government	Perfect for those who approach building a company with some "disadvantages" in their credit history and backgrounds.
Personal loans used for your business	Loan borrowed on the basis of your personal credit which you'll use toward your startup	Best for those with no previous business experience, but a strong personal credit rating.

CHAPTER 7: CONSIDER THOSE LOAD BOARDS

Whether you call it a load board or a freight board, it serves the same purpose. And as a start-up trucking company, you may find them vital to your survival. After you're established and have a customer list of your own, you'll discover you'll be less dependent on them for survival.

But you may need them for a while. There's nothing wrong with that as long as you know what it does and how to use it to get the most out of it.

The vast majority of load boards these days are quite sophisticated. They allow you to post as well as search for various loads. You can search for a wide range of types of loads, but they also allow you to narrow your search using different criteria. The load boards also provide other services for both the freight broker and the carrier.

What can you expect to find when you log onto a load board? It depends, of course, on the type of board you're using, but the most common services you'll discover include:

Matching loads
Credit information on the company – average number of days they take to pay

Message boards
Ability to make notes on shippers and carriers

FMCSA verification
Financing pre-approved loads through factoring

Mobile access

Before you jump in to use a load board, you should be aware that the freight board market is competitive. Because of this, there are any numbers of providers available to you. The first difference you'll notice is that some of these boards and some you'll need to pay. If you should choose to use a paid service, then you'll discover that the price depends on the plan you select. Some of the boards charge upwards of $100 a month for their premium plans. Having said that, just keep in mind the adage, "you get what you pay for."

This, though, isn't always the case. In fact, all paid freight boards won't always get you the best loads. So, it seems to be a good rule of thumb that you should shop around before you make a choice. This is no small choice in the early days of your business.

As you continue with your company and you find your cash flow improving as well as your own customer list growing, there may come a time when you're forced to ask the question, "Are free load boards worth your time and effort?"
Yes, it's one of those trick questions that only you can answer. It seems like using these is crucial if you

have money tied up in your start-up costs. But there'll come a time when you'll have to step back and review the big picture.

Luckily, this isn't necessarily an either-or question. Certain paid boards will offer you free trials. Here's a wonderful method to check out the board. Use the services so you can decide whether the fee they're asking is worth the cost in your current situation.
It's wise to sign up at a minimum of two at the same time. In this way, you can see what happens when the boards go head-to-head, so to speak. You're searching to see which board with all of its bells and whistles, brings you the best loads and of course, the most money from these loads.

One alternative to consider is signing up for free trials on a few paid boards. Compare them against the value that you get from free boards and determine which one is best for you and your business.

The following list of load boards are paid boards that offer free trials. It might be worthwhile to check out their services, see which ones would be best for you and give them a try.

http://DirectFreight.com/home

http://Getloaded.com

http://TruckersEdge.net

http://123Loadboard.com

http://Dat.com

http://LoadLift.us

http://Loadmatch.com

http://LoadSolutions.com

What you should know before you even use these free trials, is to consider the fact that most free load boards basically will cover all the same loads. This means you'll find that these boards have quite a bit of overlap. Don't be surprised when you go through the free boards to find this. No, it isn't your imagination.

This stands in contrast to paid boards. They list loads that are exclusively listed with them. Of course, you'll find less competition for these loads because not as many truckers use them.

The bottom line is that you need to research and use your best judgment to find a board that not only fits your freight needs but also your budget as well.

You also need to keep in mind that load boards have both benefits and drawbacks. This is why I mentioned earlier that if you're using one of these in your early stages of your company to approach potential customers then make sure to start building your own list.

The biggest advantage is that they may very well be a lifeline to a budding trucking company, such as yours. But, the largest disadvantage is the ferocious competition you'll meet on these boards.

INVOICES AND LOAD BOARDS

Today, load boards are more sophisticated than ever before. Many of these boards incorporate work with those companies that provide freight-bill factoring. This means that you can finance slow-paying freight bills. This can be a lifesaver when you're starting up or for those times when you know you're low on funds.

Other boards offer advances for fuel and other expenses. In this way, you have money in hand in order to actually take the load. Previously many drivers had to pass on certain loads which not only matched their company profile but were quite lucrative for their business.

While this may be just what your company needs at the moment, they also come with a hefty price at times. Be aware of this and use them with discretion. Make sure if you do use them you can make a good profit margin even using these services.

When you first start out, you may want to stick with free load boards. That's understandable. You're looking at the big picture of your company's expenses, and at the moment they may look monumental. Don't panic. The longer you're in the business, the expenses won't appear to be so monstrous.

Many new truckers start their businesses by looking for loads online. Load boards have advantages because they let you find loads quickly and effectively. It's an easy way to get the business rolling. Since new truckers often have tight budgets, using a free service is a good way to get some loads and save some money.

Many of these boards are regularly updated and routinely include with TL, or truckload as well as TLT, less than truckload. Shippers post loads for dry box freight, flatbed, containerized as well as reefer.

Below is a short list of some of the free load boards. It helps if you've never used one, to at least be somewhat familiar with the names of the boards.

http://CheckFreightBroker.com

http://DSSLN.com

http://FreightFinder.com

http://LandstarBroker.com

http://LiveLoads.com

http://UsaCanadaLoadUp.com

http://ReferaTruck.com

http://Trulos.com

CHAPTER 8: FREIGHT IS FREIGHT: OR IS IT?

This may seem a bit obvious, but the obtaining of freight is the most important aspect of the trucking business. But before you go much farther in your planning, you should decide what type of freight you'd like to haul.

This decision may be made a bit easier for you if, before you make a final decision, you discover a few things through your research. First, part of your decision depends on what type of freight is readily available to you.

From there you'll need to calculate how much freight you must haul in order to keep your trucks busy.

And then, you must determine the type of equipment you must acquire in order to get the job done.

As you narrow this down, the facts about this freight will help pinpoint the region in which you'll be operating. What I mean by this is you must decide if you'd prefer to run strictly in your local area, or would you rather run regionally. Finally, have you considered running your trucks cross country?

If you haven't noticed yet, these decisions are all interdependent. So, one of the thoughts you must keep in mind that wherever you send your truckers that it's in a location where they can leave that area with another load.

In other words, you have to make sure you make the best use of your trucks and your drivers. Besides, drivers make no money when they run without a load. You do that too many times, and you'll find you'll be losing some of your best drivers.

Here's a great example of how you'll need to approach a decision on your loads.

A friend of mine had the following decision to make within weeks of starting his trucking business. Flatbed loads going from Chicago to Denver were paying between two dollars and $2.20 a mile. In contrast, hauls going from Chicago to Dallas were paying $1.69 to $1.90.

On the surface, it would appear that this was an easy choice. Take the loads to Denver. But then he dug a bit more and discovered that once he got his driver into Denver, there might not be available loads to get him out of there with a load. There were only 45 loads out of Denver, but there were 131 loads out of Dallas, with higher rates.

The lesson here is that when evaluating the potential profits from your loads, you need to analyze both the load itself and the destinations. Just because you see a higher-paying load going to one market, doesn't mean you can keep that momentum going on the ride back. When you make that decision to accept a load, you need to fill it and find one that was just as lucrative as the one prior to it.

You can see that the importance of scheduling loads is not a one-way street. You or your drivers aren't going to make any money if they have to deadhead back to Chicago.

In evaluating whether a load is profitable you have to stop thinking about single loads, but about a second load once you drop the first off. That means you'll need to know your costs per mile as well as your break-even point.

In discerning this, you must factor in your trucking expenses – both your operating ones right along with those fixed expenses. I have a friend who repeats something he calls the "truckers' mantra." "There is no such thing as an unpaid mile."

A Few More Words about Loads

Below are just a few abbreviations may discover are bantered around in the trucking business when talking about loads.

LTL

This stands for less than a truckload. This is by far the most common way most trucks run. An LTL usually weighs about 8,000 pounds. The least expensive to ship, the average delivery time for this is usually between three to seven days.

TL

This refers to a truckload. Obviously, this type of load weighs more than 8,000 pounds. If you run a truckload, you'll need more space than an LTL. For the most part, the truck that picks up a truckload delivers it.

AIR RIDE TRUCKLOAD

An air ride is essential when your trucks are moving a load that can't be excessively shaken or moved too much. If you deliver this type of load, you can expect to be paid more than your average load. Because of its cost, you probably won't run into it often.

AIR FREIGHT

You'll use this type of shipment with dense weight. This type of load costs less than an LTL.

EXPEDITED FREIGHT SERVICES

This is a load with a short delivery time. You need to deliver it right away. In some industries, it's referred to as just-in-time deliveries. There can be the expensive consequence if it doesn't get to its location on time.

WHAT ABOUT YOUR COMPETITION?

At this point, you need to sit back, take a breather and give some consideration to what your competition is doing. This is extremely important when you're thinking about acquiring a contract from a potential client.

Knowing as much as you can about your competition will help you fully understand what's involved in servicing your niche as well as how you can go about obtaining a new contract.

A common mistake made by novice owners of trucking companies is that in this situation you're the only firm trying to acquire that client's business.

Realistically, there are usually several firms vying for this business.
So, who else would have his eye on this client?

For the most part, you'll encounter two types of competition. The first is your direct competition. This is a firm which is offering the same type or a fairly similar product as you do.

Your indirect competition are different services to the same potential customer.

CHAPTER 9: THE DAILY ADMINISTRATION OF YOUR TRUCKING COMPANY

Don't fool yourself. We've talked extensively so far about getting loads to haul. And there's no doubt about it. You can't make money unless you're moving freight. But you also know a well-run office, holding the fort down, so to speak, back home, is an essential aspect of any trucking business. Yours is no different.

If you analyzed a well-run trucking firm, you'd discover that it's sectioned into several major categories. These include safety coordinator, broker, sales representatives and a dispatcher. If you're going to fill these positions, then you need to have some idea of what these jobs involve.

THE SAFETY COORDINATOR

The safety coordinator is responsible for adhering to all Department of Transportation (DOT) regulations. In addition, his or her job also entails maintaining, records for your trucking firm, trailers, and the company in general.

The person in this position is expected to stay up-to-date about any changes in the regulations, especially those that may alter the current operating procedures of your drivers. So, it should come as no surprise to you that your safety coordinator not only maintains drivers' records but notifies them of random drug tests.

But wait, that's not all. The safety coordinator updates rules and regulations according to DOT and FMCSA in addition to maintaining the records of drivers' licenses and vehicles.

When DOT shows up unexpectedly at your door (Hello, it's a surprise inspection!), your safety coordinator is the point of contact. You'll not only want to hire someone who is detailed oriented but someone who won't waffle on adhering to the safety regulations.

You'll probably want an individual in this position who can stay cool under pressure. It will be a godsend if you have some idea already about the nature of the position and its importance to you and your overall business.

THE FREIGHT BROKER

There's one thing you probably already know about the trucking business, but it bears to be mentioned over and over again. Once you accept a load, barring a natural disaster, you absolutely must deliver it on time. Not only does your company's reputation depend on that, but that load could cost the company that is expecting it big bucks. In some cases, a missed or delayed load could even shut down the production of a plant. Your broker is the liaison between your company and the firm with freight that needs to be moved.

A broker's job is to find dependable alternative carriers to take the freight overflow that you may find you have now and again. This is what he does on your behalf. Let's say that there's a load worth $3,000.

He needs to broker the load out because his own company is short of trucks. His goal is to negotiate a price suitable to all parties to pick up that load and get it to its destination on time, hopefully at a price where your company doesn't take a total loss on it.

The driver of the firm the broker is negotiating with will either accept this offer or continue to negotiate another price. They agree on a rate.

SALES REPRESENTATIVE

There is no position perhaps that is more vital to your company's growth. Do you remember when we discussed the load boards? As part of the discussion, we continued to talk about the need to free yourself from being a slave to those boards by cultivating your own customer list. You'll end up with steadier work and more lucrative loads.

This is the position that can make that happen. Your sales representative searches for potentially lucrative customers. He does this through cultivating a relationship with other companies. It's not an easy job, and it may take a while for him to entice firms to use your trucking company as a carrier.

In order to do this, he may need to treat the customer to an occasional lunch or dinner out. Very often at a dinner or lunch is the place where the most progress is made in getting a new customer. In other words, don't expect your sale representative to start growing your company customer base quickly.

As your representative, he'll speak frankly with these individuals, telling them how many loads you can handle for them at the moment.

Eventually, if he can negotiate freely and successfully, the two of them will decide on the number of loads as well as the rates you'll receive. They'll sign a contract outlining the details.

From here, the sales representative sends the information to your broker. He scrutinizes to see if your firm can cover it all and if you can't immediately begin to negotiate the overflow out.

What happens when your broker can't find another firm to take a load? It certainly can't go uncovered. If that should occur, then your broker will place that load on the load board and open it up to many drivers.

THE DISPATCHER

You knew we'd get to this position sooner or later. This is another valuable position, which needs to be filled by an individual who is not only detailed-oriented but is also easy-to-work with.

Your dispatcher keeps track of all of your drivers, equipment, and loads. Here's an example of what the dispatcher does for you.

He receives information about a load that needs to be delivered. They assign this to a driver in that area, either through the radio transmission or cell phone. The dispatcher makes himself available to your drivers at all times. He is the drivers' go-to person should he have a problem with equipment, cargo or closed highways due to inclement weather.

In addition to keeping track of all your loads, drivers and equipment, the person who fills this position also maintains drivers' work records. The dispatcher may discover he's on call twenty-four hours a day. He also needs to know how to use large boards in order to keep track of the routes your drivers are taking at any one time.

The dispatcher's position is no small job. Your dispatcher will coordinate the pickup as well the delivery of your loads. If you have long-haul drivers, it's the dispatcher who will maintain the hours of service.

Larger trucking firms have more than one dispatcher. Each is assigned specific geographic area.

Most dispatchers, you'll discover, are former truck drivers themselves, but that's not always the case. Many times, dispatchers are college graduates. But a degree isn't required for this position.

The advantage to having a former trucker as a dispatcher seems obvious. He already knows the ropes. A dispatcher with this background knows exactly what your drivers are dealing with. Not only that, but he is able to calculate your drivers' times and dispatch them in a timely manner.

At times, if a dispatcher doesn't come from this background may cause some problems between himself and your drivers. That's not to say you necessarily need to steer clear of these individuals. Today, thanks to the internet, you can give your dispatchers training. Very often these training blocks are free. But even if you have to pay for training, consider it an investment well spent.

CHAPTER-10: MAINTENANCE OF YOUR TRACTOR

Keeping each of your trucks, trailers and other equipment safe and mechanically problem-free is no small job. Without a doubt, you need some method of maintaining this equipment. Not only that, DOT regulations require that your company equipment be inspected routinely. This just about requires that you have a shop–regardless of how small–for this work to occur.

If your drivers work for you and aren't owner-operators, then keeping the equipment up to DOT standards falls within your purview. At the very least you should be able to change light bulbs and tires and fill and refill fluids.

What would you do if any larger problem pops up? This is the time to turn to another larger maintenance company. There are firms who specialize in answering roadside calls from drivers who need their truck repaired. When thinking about maintenance, it's not a bad idea to cover it all and search for an on-call service as well as your own maintenance shop.

What's involved in "maintaining" your trucks? First and foremost, you want your vehicles to stay in good working condition. By inspecting them regularly, you're not only following DOT regulations, but it's a great way to perform preventive maintenance. And speaking of DOT, you must keep these records current and the trucks problem free. The last thing you need is that DOT inspection visit where they shut down some or all of your equipment.

DO YOU NEED A SHOP ON YOUR PREMISES?

That's decision only you can make. To help you, these are just a few of the activities that will take place in the shop. The first aspect to look at the size of your company as well as what type of freight you haul.

If you decide you need a shop, then you must decide on the extent of the repairs your mechanics can handle. Here are just a few of the troubleshooting and repairs that your facility can do.

Your shop will be responsible for the thirty-, ninety-, and one-hundred-twenty-day inspections. It will also be able to perform minor repairs, including such acts as tire replacement, lights, and light mechanical problems.

This facility should also be able to perform some major repairs as well, including those to engines and engine replacement as well as bodywork and paint. It's imperative that the mechanics who you hire for this facility are all certified through Automotive Service Excellence (ASE).

How Many Mechanics Do You Need?

The number of mechanics you have working in the shop depends on the number of trucks you own. It's a rough rule of thumb, but you'd be safe if you have one mechanic for every five trucks.

Stocking your repair shop also depends on how extensive repairs you're planning to be done there. Let's face it; you won't need engine parts if you only plan on making inspections and minor repairs.

But you do want to stock it with tires and windshields, as well as replacement lights for both cabs and trailers. Don't worry about maintaining an inventory. It could get complicated depending on the number of trucks, but it needn't be that difficult. If you went online, you would discover any number of software that can help you keep your inventory straight.

DOT Inspections

We've made references to a surprise inspection by the Department of Transportation. Make no mistake about it; these surprise visits strike fear into everyone at your office. The government agency will leave no stone unturned. If there's an infraction to be found, the representatives from this agency will find it.

It's difficult to go through one of these inspections and not feel at least a small pang of hurt and believe, at least for a fleeting moment that DOT is out to get you personally. That's not the case. However, keep in mind that these individuals are only doing their job. A large truck can be a rolling safety violation if not maintained properly.

If you're already involved in the business, then you're already well aware of the costs involved in the discovery of safety violations. It's not an exaggeration to say that the violations and tickets may total to thousands of dollars.

With the new CSA 2010, the violations count against the safety record of not only your driver but your company as well. For example, if your driver is stored with an over-weight load at the weigh scale that involves a ticket, the driver won't be allowed to leave until the ticket is paid.

DOT requires that maintenance and inspection records are maintained on every piece of equipment your company owns. This file must include not only the VIN or vehicle identification number, the company unit number as well as the year, make, model and tire size. This file includes all repairs made on the truck.

The other aspect of this maintenance of records is that it must remain with the carrier for 18 months. This is regardless of whether the truck is in service or not at the moment.

CHAPTER 11: YOU AND YOUR DRIVERS: HOW TO HIRE AND HOW TO KEEP THEM

No other aspect is as daunting to most individuals starting a trucking company as hiring drivers. Of course, drivers are the ones hauling the freight. You require a lot out of them. If you're going to own a company that runs cross country, you're asking your drivers, first and foremost, to spend a week or more at a time away from their homes.

And you're asking them to do it on time and even more than that, you require they follow all safety rules. And you're trusting them with your big rig. Novice owners are rightly nervous. But take a deep breath and trust your intuition, then check out some of the methods you can use to hire and retain the best, safest drivers in the business.

DON'T BE AFRAID TO USE THE INTERNET

In these cyber-days, there's no reason not to turn to the internet, at least for a bit of help. You'll be surprised at the number of recruiting tools that are available that weren't even within your reach fifteen or twenty years ago that considered routine today.

Before you go search job sites and other places drivers "hang out" on the web, turn to your own website. Drivers are searching for jobs, are without a doubt searching trucking company's websites.

Make it known on your site that you're searching for the best, then make it as easy as possible for them to send you their resume or fill out an application. If you haven't set up a Facebook page do it before you hire any more drivers. Believe it or not, this may be one of your more powerful tools in attracting drivers.

DON'T EMBELLISH THE JOB

Don't build up the job of driving for your company to sound like it's working for Google. At the end of the day when your drivers look in the mirror, they will still be truck drivers. One company owner is quite honest with his potential drivers. All he says is two words: "New Jersey."

Once they know all the facts – good and bad – drivers are able to make an intelligent decision and make some challenging decisions, but in the end, they won't feel as if they were tricked into signing on.

MAKE THEM FEEL "WELCOME."

During your driver's orientation period, make sure your new drivers feel welcome, wanted and well-respected. In other words, welcome them to the "family." When drivers, and quite frankly owners, too, hear the word "orientation," they think of a boring day of reading over procedures, rules, and regulations. But it doesn't have to be that way.

Orientation is your chance at showing them that they're going to be treated with the respect they need. It's also a chance to get them to meet those individuals they'll be interacting with on a daily basis.

I have a friend who makes sure that the fleet managers not only meet each driver in his fleet individually, but they also have a private one-on-one lunch, so the two of them can get to know each other better. The new driver also spends half a day with the maintenance manager.

One of the saddest statistics in driver attrition is that most of the turnover occurs during the first sixty to ninety days after his or her hire date. One of the new methods some truck owners are doing is pairing up new drivers with experienced mentors for that initial period.

In my questioning of other truck owners, some of them swear by the "buddy system." This means that every new driver is paired with a driver experienced with the firm to walk them through all the paperwork, help him to get better acquainted with the fleet manager, and basically just get the overall feeling for the company.

Those who have tried it say that it not only provides your new driver with a sense of belonging, but it strengthens the same feeling with the mentor. Now that's a win-win situation.

On the surface, you would think that the more you can pay your drivers, you'll attract the nation's best. And to a certain extent, you're right. But that doesn't seem to be the only factor that affects a driver's satisfaction in his job. What many drivers say they want is what is referred to as a "total work environment."

What's that? It is salary as well as health and other benefits, balanced work and personal life and a chance at improving personal development. Sounds like a tall order for a fledgling trucking company to fulfill.

Here are a few factors that may help you not only attract top-notch drivers but retain for longer periods of time.

DEVELOP MORE SOPHISTICATED PAY PACKAGES

I just said that money isn't the sole reason drivers stay in their occupation, but you'd be naïve if you believe it's not important to them. Consider as part of their hire package as a reward when they exhibit behaviors that contribute to your company's bottom line, including fuel mileage to "hard-braking" incidents to even improved inspection reports.

Some owners of trucking companies see a clear correlation between their most professional and dependable drivers and the amount of weekly take-home pay. In some companies, those type of drivers can earn more than $63,000 yearly.
Sometimes more pay isn't as important as predictable pay. Some fleets have started offering a minimum guaranteed number of miles each week.

ASK YOUR DRIVERS WHAT THEY CONSIDER IS IMPORTANT

The only sure way to know what your drivers would like as a perk in the employment is to ask them. Seems far too easy, now doesn't it? So many truck company owners begin on making improvements to their facilities or rewriting their bonus system, without having serious conversations with the drivers.

How do you go about doing this?

One way to discover what would make your drivers content in their job is by setting up a "driver advisory council." Thanks to the internet, you can reach them online, using some of the inexpensive online surveys. These tools are easy to use. Some of the best are SurveyMonkey and SurveyGizmo. Ask their opinions about possible new routes or new runs that are coming up.

You should also ask them for help in inventing new incentive plans. Find out what they think would make their job even more attractive. While you may find some totally infeasible suggestions, you're just as likely to discover some great ideas you never thought of.

If you ask your drivers for their opinions and suggestions and are only able just to enact one, imagine how they would feel when they believe their voices are heard.

CHAPTER 12: THE FUEL CARD

If you've never been a driver and used a fuel card, then you may not be familiar with this necessity. Even if you've been a trucker and using one of these for what seems like forever you may not have a full understanding of how this card works.

In any case, it really is the lifeline of your trucking company.

Believe it or not, for each dollar a trucking company makes, it actually spends 95.2 cents on operating costs. That leaves you with only a profit of 4.8 cents.

Your firm barely makes a nickel for every dollar it brings in.

This means that you need to find ways to save money. It's only natural, giving the trends of the last several decades to look at your fuel costs first.

This is where your obtaining a membership to a fleet fuel card can help your bottom line. A fuel card, contrary to what some individuals believe, is more than just a credit card. Before you commit to anyone membership, it's imperative you know how they work, doing your research now, can save you heartbreak and money down the road later.

The average customer for a fuel card is a trucking business that participates in over-the-road runs and buys its diesel for their class 7 and class 8 commercial trucks from truck stops. Designed to benefit carriers who run from one to literally hundreds of rigs, you'll discover a wide variety of firms benefiting from them, including carriers, private fleets, less-than-load (LTL) carriers as well as independent owner-operators.

Carriers benefit from a good fuel card program with its discounts on every gallon of diesel, sometimes as much as two to three percent. The exact amount of savings may be slightly different from one truck stop to another depending on the settlement the merchant negotiated with the card company. One important aspect you need to seriously consider is whether you can actually use the card along the lanes your company does.

The fuel card companies use two models of savings. The first is called "retail-minus" and the second is "cost-plus." The retail-minus model is just as it positions itself to be. A specific amount of money is deducted from the price of each gallon of fuel bought. And then that savings is passed to the fuel card customer.

The second model, cost-plus is a bit more complicated. The savings determined at each fuel location by an independent agency which is known as Oil Pricing Information Service of OPIS. This agency calculates the base or "rack" price of fuel for each individual location. It takes the base price and adds in taxes as well as transportation costs in these locations. OPIS then adds other fees.

Just listening and reading this casually, you would expect this second alternative would be more expensive than the first. In reality, it's actually less expensive in some states, especially in California and Hawaii. Then there are a few fuel cards that try to give you the maximum savings depending on the circumstances at the location you pump.

By this, I mean it gives you what some individuals call the "better off" choice. The card automatically selects which of the two pricing models provide you with the better savings. In this way, fleets and drivers alike don't have to worry about switching between the two-retail minus or cost-plus choices. When the fuel card has the ability to recognize the difference and calculate the best for you, you can feel reassured you're getting the best deal of all.

How does Fuel Card work?

Some companies will charge you a small, fixed fee for each transaction your firm makes when it purchases diesel. You could receive your savings immediately at the pump, or they may send you a check at specific times of the year.

In addition to that, some merchants may offer what's referred to point-of-sale discounts. These discounts actually lower the cost of the fuel when you pay. This means the fleet pays the lower price to the fuel card company and then the fuel card company reimburses that lower cost to the merchant.

Not every merchant prefers that method, though, and that's where the rebate model comes into play. In this way, the fleet pays for the full cost of the fuel, and you'll receive a check at the end of a certain time period, usually a month, for the total amount of money that had been discounted. This can confuse some drivers who think that they aren't receiving the discounts promised in the card.

Perks of Fuel Cards

You may never have thought to investigate it, but believe it or not, using a fuel card can provide your trucking firm with several other benefits. Below are just a few of the ways it can help your bottom line.

Keeping Fuel Expense under control

Some cards offer you weekly lines of credit and a program called PlusCheks. With these two provisions, your drivers can also pay for expenses incurred over-the-road. Each fleet has the ability to limit the amounts the drivers spend using fuel cards, which then reduces the chances of fraud.

Not only that, but these programs are safer to use than handing your drivers an unrestricted credit card or a certain amount of cash to use

Managing Your Fleet

Depending on the fuel card you use, you may discover a program which allows you to view the online accounts that are real-time and detailed reports of every transaction. In addition to that benefit, you can customize these reports so you can actually tell which drivers are spending the most on fuel, which retailers offer the best details. Armed with this information, you can operate your fleet cost-efficiently.

What you do with this information is up to you, but some of the ways it can be used are to monitor, score and compare drivers' behaviors. You're able to pinpoint not only the routes but the fuel stops themselves that offer the best savings for your fleet. Not only that, but this can help when you submit your fleet's quarter IFTA filings.

IMPROVE YOUR COMMUNICATION

Everyone is all too accustomed to the daily fluctuations in fuel prices. Because of this, it's vital that your firm works with a fuel card company that allows you to discover the latest fuel discounts within its networks. To this end, you may find that certain cards actually offer cell phone apps – applications –

that allows your drivers to identify the lowest prices in the location where your drivers are.

This can be not only cost saving but time savings as well. It means you need to spend less time in planning routes in addition to eliminate the worry of overpaying at the pump.

MISCELLANEOUS SAVINGS

While you may choose a fuel card for the fuel savings itself, as you research your choices these are just a few other perks you may find. But they aren't the only ways. You'll find more as you dig deeper into the difference among these cards.

Don't be surprised if you find you can also save money on maintenance costs, tire prices, and other repairs, and even on lodging.
And when you're looking at less than a nickel profit for every dollar you make, any legitimate savings are welcome.

CHAPTER 13: MARKETING YOUR TRUCKING COMPANY

product
price
the marketing mix
promotion
place

A trucking company is not much different than any other firm, especially in regards to marketing. You can't expect to open your doors thinking that magically people will find you.

You'll need to advertise and market your firm to let people know you're the new truck in town and you're ready to deliver their loads, on time and safely. There are many ways to do this, not the least of which is the internet. To be fully effective at letting people know you're in business; you'll need to do a combination of both offline and online marketing. In a way, you're in the perfect position for offline advertising.

As a trucker already, you're in all the places truckers and brokers and owner-operators gather. You have an audience as it were, just sitting there. It's an advertiser's dream come true. You're not tied down to one geographic location in your "networking" efforts, as so many of those opening new businesses are.

Of course, some trucking companies started purely by word of mouth, but there are various actions you can take to supplement that without spending much money.

If you're perplexed at what your first step should be, why not just consider your business card as a marketing tool. If you've ever had business cards made for any reason, you know that the more you buy, the less expensive they are. And you should have your hands full of these cards.

If you're an over-the-road driver now, think of what could happen if you left your business cards at local bulletin boards that truckers and brokers frequent.

Ask at restaurants you eat at if they will let you leave a few cards on their counters, any small bookstores, new shops or even lottery kiosks will let you put a few out. You never know who may pick one up. But seriously, think about it, it's not like you're going to run out of the cards anytime soon.

A great way to expand that type of advertising is by harnessing the power of a well thought out and well-written brochure. With a brochure, you get the chance to tell your company's "story" in some detail. A brochure gives you room to tell your potential customers what your business does, your location or locations if you have more than one.

If you don't feel comfortable writing it, you can hire someone who will write for a surprisingly small fee. And just like your business cards, a brochure can be disbursed in a wide variety of places, from supermarkets to truck stops, restaurants, as well as rest stops, and hotels.

DIRECT MAIL ADVERTISING

Really? Really . . .

For those of you who thought that direct mail advertising rode off into the sunset on the back of a dinosaur, think again.

Direct marketing can be a valuable tool in establishing your presence in a niche market. All it takes is customized direct mail campaign. You start by finding a broker of those who rent companies' names and addresses. In your case, you may want to specifically send this campaign to auto parts manufacturers based in a specific geographical regional market.

Write a sales letter or have a direct mail copywriter draft the letter to send to the potential customers. Some firms send out informative postcards. This is a good way to offer some type of discount or deal for new customers. In other words, you'll have to give the firms on the list a reason to give you a try.

When you're building your direct mail campaign, be sure to include all of the addresses. This gives individuals another quick and easy way to connect with you.

Yes, use social media too!

So far in the twenty-first century, no more powerful internet marketing tool has emerged than Facebook. As much as you may not like the idea, internet marketing is here to stay, whether through Facebook or some next big tool. And your firm needs to be there. Use the various tools, from Facebook to Twitter, Instagram, and other social media utensils.

The advantage, let's say, creating and having a Facebook fan page is that you're connecting with customers at a entirely new level. Unlike direct mail, you can get to know your customer better, and they can learn things about it. The relationship becomes a close professional relationship with a personal touch. There's something to think about.

WHY ARE YOU MARKETING?

That may seem like a strange question, but it really isn't. And it'll make more sense to you if we ask instead, "What is your objective in marketing?"

Marketing is a wonderful and a supremely lucrative activity, but if you don't have a clear motive behind it, then you're more than likely to be disappointed in the outcome.

In other words, before you even begin marketing your firm, know what your goals are. For some firms, especially fledgling ones, it's to build a customer base, sometimes from the ground up.

So far, we've been talking about one objective, and that's building a solid customer base. But, remember sooner or later you'll find yourself in search of good, seasoned drivers. This marketing plan will need an entirely different structure.

OBJECTIVE #1: BUILDING A CUSTOMER BASE

I've mentioned this before, that so many of the factors you use in determining what type of trucking business you'd like to own are interdependent. The equipment you buy depends on the loads you'd prefer to haul, which in turn depends on the types of clients you're searching for.

Now, that we've talked about loads and equipment, we'd be remiss if we didn't say a word or two about the type of customer you'd like to attract. Choosing clients is too important to leave just to intuition. You can give your intuition some help by doing your homework.

When you have a clear vision of your target client, then you'll have a clear perspective on what you really want. And with that, you can then develop a plan to find them.

Listed below are just a few of the ways you'll hear some business owners describe their perfect client. While this isn't saying it's yours, it might get you started thinking about what's important to you.

A large, well-established shipper
Pays on time
Pays well
Has a good reputation
Is loyal about giving you his loads
Provides you with shipments that fit the lanes you want to drive

FINDING WELL-PAYING SHIPPERS

Once you've defined and envisioned your perfect client, you'll need to find him. You'd be surprised at how easy this could be. One of the most common ways to find a lucrative customer is through an industry association. Check your area to see if there are any local chapters in your area.

Just to give you a clue, I'm not referring about a trucking association. You'll find plenty of competitors, but no clients. No, I'm talking about associations your ideal clients belong to. If you're looking for potential retail store clients, then you should find a local association of retailers. Ideally, see if you can join the group.

Similarly, if you want to specialize in car hauling, then you should try to join organizations and association that deal with automobile dealerships.

Just about every industry has an association to help forward the welfare of that industry. When you're doing this, think out of the box. It's easy to come up with the common industries.

You can bet your bottom dollar that your competitors are looking at these as well. So take your time, do some brainstorming and mind-mapping and dig into the less common industry. When you do this, you might be welcomed with open arms. These smaller groups are sometimes under-served by the trucking industry.

When you begin to search for the associations of other industries, you may find that you aren't eligible to join, since you aren't in their industry. But by asking the right questions, you can still join. While you probably won't get all the rights and privileges of a full member, you'll still get what you really want: accessibility to that group of customers.

Many of these groups have members with partial rights. They're usually called "corporate" members or even "related industry" members. That's you. And that's the way you meet these business owners. Barring this, you should also be aware that many of these groups have lists of membership which they may be willing to give to you. The information on these lists usually includes the members' names, their contact numbers as well as their email addresses. If you do receive a list like this, handle it with discretion. Use it in a professional manner.

Once you make contact, either as a member or with a list of the members, you can now roll up your sleeves and dig in to do the real work of searching for your ideal customer.

Your next step is to sell yourself. People find it much easier to sell friends or their supervisors. As a society, we're not very good at selling ourselves. But that's exactly what you're about to do. Call the names on the list. This list has now become your prospective client list. Ask to speak to the person in charge of shipping. Your goal is to set up a meeting to discuss your mutual needs. If you can't reach the person you need to in this manner, then you send them a letter.

Your goal is to find out not only how they select their carriers but how you could get on that list.
If you've chosen to be a company that specializes in moving families cross-country to their new homes, you'll have a different marketing object – some slightly different wording – than if you're searching to get in touch with brokers who may need a dependable company on their list when they find themselves in need.

HAVE YOU THOUGHT ABOUT THE GOVERNMENT?

That's right. Have you thought about being a carrier for the U.S. government? Perhaps you should.

Believe it or not, it can be a great client. The government has a lot of freight that needs to be moved, pays well as well and has the ability to provide your company with regular work. These contracts, by the way, aren't easy to obtain but could turn out to be well worth the effort. It's something to think about.

Consider, for a moment, how much money your business could make if your firm were able to move freight for the postal service. Possibly a company such as Amazon can use you to deliver their packages. You'd have a secure job – to say the least. If that doesn't appeal to you why not attempt to get your business listed with the GSA.

There are also many opportunities to haul military freight as well.

NEW CUSTOMERS AND YOUR CASH FLOW

We've mentioned it before in connection with acquiring new customers, but it bears repeating anytime we talk new customers. It's a hazard of starting a trucking company. You may find that many of your new customers pay their bill within 30 to 60 days.

That translates into a least a thirty-day lag. If you were an established firm with positive cash flow and a reserve of money, this wouldn't affect you as much. But it can be a hassle for you. So just be careful, and think the entire scenario through before you enter into any contract with a new customer.

OBJECTIVE #2: ATTRACTING DEPENDABLE DRIVERS

This objective needs a different focus. If this is your objective, you actually have to devise an entirely new game plan. If you're at all remotely familiar with the trucking industry, then you already know that it a frighteningly high turnover rate. Even the respected website CNN Money has commented on this,

One owner said he got so frustrated searching for drivers that when he did market for even one or two to add to his fleet, he made the following goal, "Find a dozen drivers who will submit an application, provide copies of the CDL license and sign contracts to provide driving services."

The point being is that he's hiring a number of drivers at once, perhaps more than what he needs because he's well aware of the attrition rate in this area.

What Kind of Costs Am I Looking At?

Starting a trucking company that can be expensive, there's no way to sugar-coat it. But if you can find investors to help, you can dive into one of the most lucrative businesses in the nation. It's well worth the cost and energy you place into your startup.

So, don't let the sticker-shock of some of these costs scare you off. If you hear the trucking industry calling your name, chances are you'll be successful in your endeavor if you listen.

According to some experts the start-up costs can range from $6,000 to $15,000. Of course, as with everything else in the trucking industry, the costs depend on several factors, not the least of are the type of freight you decide to haul and the type of equipment you purchase.

Beyond that, though, several other factors may influence your initial costs. These could be the states in which you run, and whether you lease or own your trucks. Below is a quick table of a few of the major costs. Yours may be less or more. But at least it gives you an idea.

Item	Cost
Formation and registration documents	$900-15,000
Insurance Down Payment for each truck	$2,000-$4,800
IRP – apportioned plates per truck	$500-$3,000
Heavy Vehicle Use Tax and other permits	$100-$550
Additional State-Specific or other permits	$500

GETTING YOUR OWN AUTHORITY

If you're already an owner-operator, then you undoubtedly already have your authority. But if you're a company driver, it's your employer that's holding the authority.

So, exactly what is an authority? It is a permission from the Federal Motor Carriers Safety Administration (FMCSA) to haul freight for profit. You'll discover there are two types. One is a contracting authority granted to a carrier who hauls freight for businesses it has a contractual agreement with. The other is common authority allows your company to haul for any entity that has anything to be transported whether you are formally contracted with them or not.

Regardless of the type, the carrier must have a minimum of $750,000 worth of liability insurance.

CONCLUSION

As you consider launching your trucking company, you should congratulate yourself. Whether this was done knowing the immense profit potential of a trucking company – even a small one – you've chosen a solid industry.

Within this lucrative industry, you're opening yourself and eventually your employees to untold business opportunities. Niche markets are plenty. The health of the industry is verified by the number of new truck firms that are registered each year.

Don't look at that last sentence as an indication that the industry is being flooded. It's more telling of the financial vibrancy of the trucking business. A fair amount of these startup firms fail, not because there aren't profits to be made. Firms who fail usually aren't well thought out, or the owners just give up for personal reasons. Those firms that remain strong are poised for great success.

One of the best steps you can do as you continue on your journey is to scrutinize your competitors. As you scan which are the most successful firms, try to discover what makes them so successful. If there's anything you can do to replicate their success, then do it. But more than that, see if you can do what they do even better. If you do this, you're well positioned to obtain a large portion of the market share.

This book helps you at least get acquainted with just about every facet of the trucking industry, from the simple start of obtaining your CDL and ensuring your drivers have theirs to your legal options to creating a solid business structure.

In addition to these concepts, we've covered other factors you need to consider as you pull your resources together, not the least of which is a fuel card, a pertinent business plan and marketing your firm.

This information will give you a good start toward your dream. And as you dream of success consider these few statistics the speak volumes to the vibrancy of the trucking industry.

Semi-trucks are responsible for moving nearly 10.43 billion tons of freight as of 2016. Those statistics come from the American Trucking Association. That number represents nearly 80 percent of all the freight hauled in this country.

In addition to that, the US has nearly 34 million trucks registered for business purposes with some 7.5 million Americans employed in trucking-related jobs

It seems you've chosen a very lucrative and necessary industry. Congratulations!

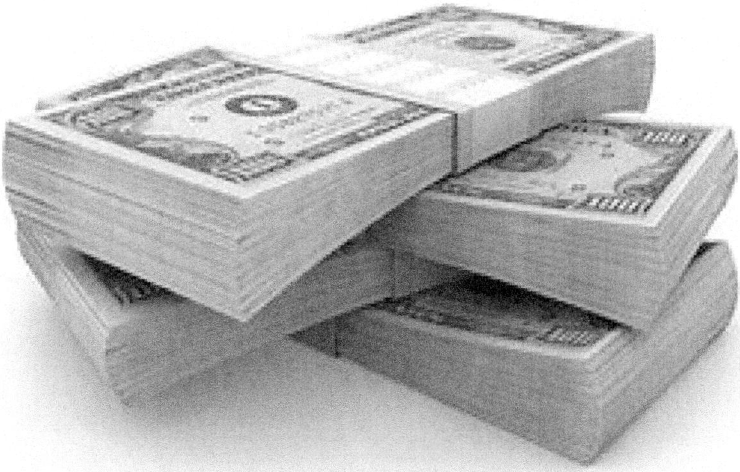